RECKONINGS

RECKONINGS

Ryan Walsh

BAOBAB PRESS

RENO, NV

First Printing

ISBN-13: 978-1-936097-23-4
ISBN-10: 1-936097-23-0

Library of Congress Control Number: 2018950308

Baobab Press
121 California Avenue
Reno, Nevada 89509
www.baobabpress.com

Printed in the United States

Cover Art: "The Night We Didn't See" by Katie Grauer
©2011 Katie Grauer

In Memory of David Budbill – Friend and Guide

CONTENTS

III

IV

Reckonings

RECKONING: n. 1. the act of counting or computing. 2. an itemized bill or statement of a sum due. 3. a settlement of accounts: a day of reckoning. 4.a. the act or process of calculating the position of a ship or an aircraft. b. the position so calculated.

Before the Word

They say
we are blowback
from the Big Bang

Stardust
and old light

Vessels of water and minerals

Hydrogen, calcium, sodium

Are we really all the things outside of us?

Magnesium, manganese, silicon

On the bus
people touch people
they don't know

feeling heartbeats
through jackets
shoulder to shoulder

but the parts don't gel

Cadmium, arsenic, zinc

The whereabouts of hearts anyway

Our moon, they say,
is a blasted hunk of earth

orphaned and orbiting

We live half-blind
like a car gliding over black ice
the driver doesn't know is black ice

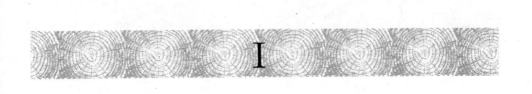

I

Appalachian Spring

Spring breaks across Appalachia.
One morning dawn light dazzles;
hens cluck in the hen house
and the backyard magnolia
froths with pink-lipped petals,
like salmon leaping fervently
against a waterfall's white hem.
Come next daybreak, grass blades
glitter in a killing frost;
the shock of scattered blossoms spreads
severed hands in mute applause.

PRUNTYTOWN

We were warned against
the barbed-wire fence. Warned

against the quick cold slice
of the creek. The horse's teeth.

Warned that certain boys were sent
to the Home down the road.

I knew then to get away.
I let it grow in my blood.

GHOST FACTORY

It is imprinted on me, the factory on the hill
(no more factory, no more hill).

Grand and silent as a church.
Rusted hulk like a breathing scab

I couldn't help but touch.
Those powder hills and slag heaps

we raced bikes over raising dust.
DuPont dismantled the smelter brick

by brick then brought down the shell.
Cadmium, arsenic, lead. Shadow

plant rooting down like a dark star
black-holing the whole town.

::

All night the ghost factory is awake
making new ghosts.

Somewhere someone else
will do this for even less.

Now wind rakes the reclaimed site
each grass blade blazing

and a family pulls from the creek
fish no one should eat.

In the Hiss of Lithe, Bright Grasses

Why can't I be
a slender stalk
wind-bent, rustling
against sisters, brothers,
braceleted wrists
of the Spirit
instead of marbled meat
and water,
unreceptive to
transmissions?

Tell me, if I sit here
stone enough
to see each leaf
of aspen tremble
in its turning
or join the water
floating,
might I too
become
bronzened
light?

THE SPLASHER FLOOR (1969)

On the splasher floor no one spoke.
You worked by the smidgy light of furnace vents,
the molten metal and cherry tips of cigarettes.

Each day a machinery of sweat:
break the clay, pour the zinc, pull the chains,
dam the trough in time. Hoist the buckets,
touch the flames, pour each ingot down the line.

Clouds rose from each of you as the dust
of the floor became greasy with fat.
A body is three-quarters water.
You evaporated by the hour,
the rivets in your jeans burning like hornets.

And the old guys had it worse, hauling
the extra pounds, those extra years darkly,
zinc at the back of your throats. Leering,
half choking, and proud of simply surviving
third shift, dangling out the fourth floor window
breathing dead light between smokes before dawn.

Hot as hell before the sun was even up.
Yet still you danced circles around
the slippery floor—with Gonzalez, Menendez,
Shingleton, and the rest—making
good at three and a quarter an hour.

ASPARAGUS

From snow pools and dark soil it rises.
Spring's scout. With rubber boots
we walk the morning field
scanning the fine light air of May.

Asparagus teaches us to see
its peculiar green (neither thistle nor pea).
Look for the shy lithe curve of its stem
like a tiny giraffe grazing on neighbors: foxtail, quackgrass.

We snap and stack them one by one in the tub
careful not to crumble their velvety heads.
Soon June brings strong sun, chard and lettuce,
sugar peas, the joyful stain of beets and strawberries.

Then the corn stalks begin to whisper. Spring's tender
shoots crushed by the bushel. Potato and summer squash.
Long days grown forgetful of winter. No more
cold mornings. No more strange waft rising
from our urine like a reminder of death.

CAULIFLOWER

We're in the west field
harvesting cauliflower.
Head stacked on head in each
crate stacked on crate in
the flatbed Luther hauls away.
I think of others who've worked
in fields all day owned by the land,
owned by other men. My heart belongs
to my friends. This morning I cracked
two eggs against the skillet
and thought of the box truck rolling
over the helmet around your brain;
and I remembered what Jared said:
you know, we're each just an egg
balanced on a spoon in one of those races.
How many heads of cauliflower would it take
to fill the emptiness of a truck like that?

I have to think about that
as I wipe the mud from my blade
and hack another brainstem stump,
picking its leaves, remembering
the Goodpasture boys so full of the urge
to swallow August whole. How
one summer they leapt from the bridge
into the green jaws of South Lake Holston
with cataclysmic beauty. Big trucks
rumbled past between Tennessee and Virginia.
I stood at the rail and watched the sticky air
they fell through, their twin splashes circling outwards.
Imagined the sound like low blue thunder
sucking them under green water then brown
then the pulverizing dark where farms drowned
when the TVA plugged the river and made islands
out of hilltops. The Goodpastures were born
divers. Still, blood trickled from his ear when
Terry shook his head, stared. *I can't hear you.*

IN THE FRAME OF INNINGS, PENDLETON COUNTY, WV

Remember it shin-deep, that coppery, sulfuric hue
the North Fork of the South Branch—

the way it caught the summer glow
and threw it back to us tarnished?

We cruised those towns along the shallow ribbon:
Petersburg, Moorefield. Wampler farms. August heat.

The summer's sweet promise grown overripe,
scudding away downstream where eagles once nested

in the high-eaved banks. Bruised stink of poultry on the air.
Our fathers' work shirts crumpled on the bedroom floors

a sweaty heap; twenty years old and nowhere to go.
Just get ahold of what you can and swing like hell, Dad said. D'ya hear me?

We were young men, old boys grown too old from work,
the Guard, the low empty skies of our homes.

Sundays we gathered at the ballpark by the swale,
at the edge of hairy cornfields, where crows swarmed

and the river's dog-legged riffles kept the beers cold.
Filling into our bodies roughly, abundantly,

we were ready to put order to the green frenzy, our randy lives
with ball and bat, the smack of knuckles on leather palms,

the hey-nana-nana of pop and fling, gulping
our fleeting youth in the frame of innings.

Around there it all floats down the Potomac, on to Washington,
someplace else. The jobs, the college-bound, the new corridor

they had to run so many off to lay—a gash
in the ridgeline marks the route.

Eminent domain, the government called it.
Farm lines redrawn. Mountains thrust aside and scarred.

Big chugging trucks headed out of state. Loss arriving
in rehearsal for departure, hauling out the pieces.

So when someone like Travis Harper
could manage to rear back and uncoil

from some sweet sovereignty of motion
a slider that swept in from the knees

and bit the heart out of the plate, you bet
I dropped my shoulder, held my stare

and followed through with all I had.
It left me slack-jawed, glazed, then smiling.

What else to do but tip my hat
and marvel at that little bit of mastery?

—a moment of perfection amid
the sloppy, high-scoring hours of those days.

Afterwards, swerving down dirt roads,
throwing dust into the gleaming night,

we pressed the pedal home.

II

FABLE

Once upon a time

there were rivers and streams

you could drink from

THE SINKS

Something in us sinks,
density of mountains
in the hip bones. We've grown
sludge-hearted, carbon-veined.
Slurry ponds rising behind our ribs.

We do not float so well,
a people raised on dark
swift rivers. There's not a lake
in West Virginia not made

by man, bulldozed and dammed,
or engineered for containment of spoil.
Trout stocked deep with cancer.

Cadmium, arsenic, lead, and zinc
leach into the tables, the water
we drink. We sink and we sink.

Send not a flood, O Lord.

LUMINARIES

She drags her cigarette and casts
ashes into the street.
A little place in the air
just off the knuckles
glows against the twilight.

She appears like the luminaries
we placed as boys around
the post office at Christmas.
Little tea candles nested
in sand in white paper bags.
We cut a star into each of them
to let the light out.

In the dusk, her gown looks
out of place. There's been some mistake.
Little flowers, a shade between sky
blue and lavender, seem too hopeful
against white cotton and the test results.
O Holy Night floats on her lips
and a few flakes drift

the way the great blue heron
now glides freely, almost invisibly,
across the parking lot to
the marsh to stand and wait
attentively for what comes next.

SELF-PORTRAIT WITH EXILE, BEARS, AND THE ORIGINAL CARTER FAMILY

All the bears in the zoo look pathetic.

Their eyes glazed, bodies lethargic.

You can shake the fence and snarl; they'll hardly flare their nostrils.

I think they are majestic.
Inhabiting their fur so far from family, so public.

I want to send them home.

::

I have walked among the bears at dusk, along the thoroughfares and
meadows of Western Carolina.

I have sown the fields as instructed.

I have waded to the far-side banks of Jordan.

Above the river, a weeping willow weeps.

::

Another day of snow down the neck.
Another day without mountains.

Thank you, Lord, for these thy gifts, the beatings we are about to
receive
from the bounty of Upper Midwestern winters.

I have rolled up my sleeves.

Who will fetch us from the long sleep?

THE FURNACES

The company would wait
and pick three men
Gonzalez, Whaley, and Medina
Kill the fires the night
was a black star
First one man lowered by rope
Blasting at the bricks
striking his body
Harness biting muscles
wrenching. Ten minutes on
Send another body down
or smoked, breathing fire
But there was no new lining
The bricks could withstand
Roasting in their skins
Josefina Alvarez smoked
while chunks of brick rained
Later, both Medina's boys
would heed the station
rushing through fires
Grandpa made a patio
after the smelter shut down
flipping burgers and feeding us
the dangers in earning your bread.
and lowered in the dark
the flames passing over

until summer, god knows why,
from the extras gang
to reline the vertical retort furnaces.
before but the mouth
remnant of a fallen sun.
harness, the jackhammer on another line.
bitten by shrapnel
wheeling in the dark rotisserie.
the damned twisting hammer
the line for each, then haul him out.
while the others caught a breath
to quell fire, waiting.
for their throats.
2,500 degrees, but a man?
like the longaniza
in her backyard
through the darkness.
and a grandson
sirens, born to ignite,
as volunteers.
from the curved yellow bricks
a place to grill meat
stories of the men he worked with
They knew what it was to be lifted again
to wrestle with the terrible angel
and to have prevailed another day.

EXPERT TESTIMONY
(PERRINE V. DUPONT, 2008)

- Dr. Kirk Brown, soil scientist

We all know that someone   something   will kill you

People   should consider   cancers   could be   failures
   Nature   children   adults   exposed
            get it on the skin   ingest it
                                          breathe   it   in
   drink it   Through careful study   we know   how much
                              children breathe
Risk   published   in   the   air
                 the milligrams
                 and cubic feet
   Calculate the method

                                                        in the air

            times concentration
                                          in your house

your lungs

                     the kidneys

   The pathways

                 and   probabilities

                        It's a standard methodology

   and I didn't include
                     lead   or
                                                        zinc

ALLOWANCE

He was prepared (weren't you?)
to do what men in that time
in that place did: sacrifice
the body in the name of pride.
Thinking somehow that melting
in the smelter steam
of his own salt cake would prove
he was better than those
who owned his time
and held him to the fire.
But where'd that get us?

New River

West Virginia dug at its veins until
something dark emerged: a shadow
that stained the hands, smudged the sky,
burst the slurry dam in our minds.
Silica, bituminous coal, opioids:
Extraction and injection.

Suspended in air, you can run
a hand along the rusty rail and look
down. Beneath the bridge, the New
River like a cold zipper. One night

in May your brother zipped himself into
a black bag. Your blue Honda ditched in the lot
at the overlook. Hands felt the rail. Frog choruses
in the distance. Will, you left the bridge
became part of the air,
part of the crazed foaming river.

I can still picture your hands worrying
the blue beads of a rosary
in the pew next to me. We confessed
we believed in all that is seen and unseen.
You are now river: cold stone and
muttering rapids and there is no
putting this darkness back underground.

SPELTER, WEST VIRGINIA (UNINCORPORATED)

It's not what you think.
DuPont owns the soiled ground.
They're on the hook for containment,
the fate and transport of contaminants,
site reclamation, health monitoring, cash settlements.

And still the bottle smash of green glass
is all that's left of the playground.
A plastic Kroger's bag caught in the chinking—
Spelter's only banner.

The rusted hulk of the smelter
and the small brick church
where some got on their knees.

This isn't unique.
Superfund towns bloom like poppies, the pox,
the beet-red cheeks of Joe Domingo,
who worked swing shifts with your uncle.
But who will recall a single fact from this place?

If they can call us white trash, then it's okay
to drink up, blot out, mine, blast, frack, and fuck
every hole and deposit. Then dump,
flush, dredge, and spoil away every bit of us,
all we have left.

Unincorporated? It was always corporate:
Ziesing, Grasselli, Matthiessen+Hegeler, DuPont.

We lived in little company houses they kept close,
wanted us to catch a glimpse on lunch break
of just what they held ransom.
As if we didn't know.

SINKS OF GANDY

Just off the Dry Fork Road
a cave
offers cover from a storm

We can't see to see

But the dark

Anything can happen
in the dark

Life in the sea-bottom sulfide
of hydrothermal vents

an upstream surge of semen
toward the fallopian tubes

the bank where the last elk
was killed

The last

::

Here

I knew that we would all
disappear
one way or another

A sleeping secret
tucked in my brain

like an aneurysm

Little black moth
waiting to take wing

BLIND LEMON SOMETHING

Once I lived a whole summer

inside a lemon. Bright bitter skies

and the salt. You had to squint

to make sense of it. Laundry

on the line and words

squeezed from the throat.

And no sugar. No sugar.

III

SAM'S GAP, TN/NC

You must be born again.
First clouds, then rain.
Then evaporation's cool hand
lifting. The horizon we see
is the horizon. Tracings
of hawk. Eyeful
of mountain like
the body of the beloved
in repose. You cannot
go home again.

PAINTING

I paint a field of snow
and a man standing in it.
That's my picture of *solitude.*

I paint a red bird in flight above the man.
His head is raised. I call that *song.*

If I paint the bird black and then another
and another until there are 5,000 blackbirds
piled on the ground, it is *the sinks.*

Perhaps snow obscures all but a couple blackbirds.
The man disappears in drifts of white and blue.

Two birds remain to share a black seed (once a bird)
in the snow crust. What do you call that?

Reckoner

The earth misses us
It hasn't rained for months

The sleek new skins of our hand-
held devices flash
like the blank face of the lake

We go down to it and bathe
in its shades: gin clear fluorescent grey

::

Sometimes we bump along
shoulder to shoulder

in a simulacrum of friendship
in its undertow

Is that you?
Seen and unseen

like a ghost man on second
like an underage labor camp

If we're not in it
where are we?

::

All our campfire girls
All our drowned fuselages and kelped wrecks
All our pine pollen soft parades

Our mouthfuls and gulped breaths
How many gigabytes is that?

::

Sometimes we float in it almost
bodiless lost in the flickering
voices that can never save us

even with all that value added

::

The touchscreen technician
who assembled and wiped
our smartbook faceplate

Her little hands ruined
by the solvents
by the rhythms

so we can share
with smudgeless clarity

::

Like little cones
raining from the pines
girls drop from factory eaves

Circles touching circles
spreading across faces

Yours mine theirs
We take we take and we tag

::

On the lakeshore a mother mallard
nestles into needles that make her
home above rocks

where a boy with a stick
is sure to find her

Where is your warm hand
for my hand?

Dark Zone in the Night Map

Our father stood at the window
staring at holes in the earth—
one for each of us.

It's true, our lives will fit
the shape of their containers
like water or sand

like West Virginia walled in by the Blue Ridge
on one hand, the Ohio and Big Sandy rivers on the other.

What if your hole was a door home?

What if everything went blind as a cave mouth in the rain?
A star zone as in old times.
Where is my hand?

Where are the lungs the world uses to keep breathing?
From space, our planet is a pale light,
a flickering pilot flame.

Creek-washed shapes
smoothed the cave floor
like calves asleep in a night pasture.

Our flashlights wobbled along the walls.
Mike Loves Emily in blue paint.
Tinfoil in a firepit.

THE LEE SHORE

I want a darkness I can remember

Here
Even this

lip of the continent
this garden of whales
this nightwater

arrives mottled like the hides of harbor seals
like the moon clouded over

It doesn't matter what I want

::

I watched the oats in the pot
breathing

like a man's chest
rising and falling as he sleeps

like the heaves of hill upon hill
making shadows in the yard

How does it feel
that last breath that turns you
into night
into ocean salt
into coral

::

Or did the twin sparrows on your chest
bear you the miles home
to the foothills

where your brothers found
black veins in the earth

new light

::

At the bottom of the sea there is no
lamp to read by

Just the memory of white lilies arranged in a milk bottle
by an open window in July

READING

When I am dry for words,
gone weeks or months without
a line, let me remember
the mosses.
        Let me take in
the filtered light of others' leaves,
cling to whatever molecule
of water they might shed
in the deep folds of my mind
until a syllable can squiggle forth
thin and vulnerable (one cell thick)
but damp with possibility.
Let the slightest dew ignite
the green, dark flame. Let it consume
rocks and tree roots, whole forests
of thought in its slow primordial burn.

"Now Comes Good Sailing . . ."

The Abenaki said
       the first moose
              was a whale.

It slimed onto the shore
       with jellyfish
              for guts.

Henry, what you said implied
       the afterlife
is loon-throated
       nights on northern lakes.

More expedient than birch canoe,
       bateaux,
              steamboat—

that final travel

along marsh cress,
       speckled alder, red osier,
              shrubby willows, sallows.

After the gun report,
       the skinning knife,
a brown and musky
velvet-boned commodity.

Hoof-pocked mud.
Silence.

Stalking something else
        in your journal, you wrote
by fire under moon
or by phosphorescent moosewood:

        Ktaadn, the highest place;
Chesuncook, where streams empty in;
        Allegash, hemlock-bark.

From your bed in Concord,
        two words made the portage
through that pine-rich dark:
        "Moose" you said, then "Indian,"

then drew a breath
        plunged down, in deep
                and crossed to the far shore.

THE CLOUD

We act as though the good days
will never cease. Like we might live
forever in a searchable mist,
while gathering tweets swallow the skies.
Tiara grins and selfies,
speculum and fire.

Do you feel more connected?

Let's not forget the cloud
is not a cloud. Ventilated
warehouses devour rivers.
Colonies of servers buzz
in their rack space,
the ceaseless hum and heat

stacked deep
like penned herds standing panicked
in their own antibiotic waste

What are you serving?

After the collapse, lost combs
grew thick with honey.
We discovered the hive
in a meadow on its side

like a black box waiting for recovery
like a fallen buffalo
gone to bone,
something ghost-given.

Whoever said it would be painless?

The cloud is a thing
we can unmake by brick
or by blast. Like any stone
thrown into a lake
or through glass,
it ripples and it reckons,
the current startled out.

Is your memory backed up?

Our brains are still
in our bodies, our hearts.
As we wade into the rolling blackouts
we'll need a human heat.

Where are your friends tonight?

A patch of roadside thistle,
clover, asters, heather—
like the weeds we'll be
when we die—
gathered and regurgitated,
transformed by the workers into sugars.

We unlatch the box
and scrape the dusk
from our frames—the dead wings,
each cell a tiny flood—

and watch the final oozings
for hours, this dark remaining
joy we take into our brief bodies.

DAY OF RECKONING

What if it's like this

snow day

instead of mayhem

tranquil

like a pillow

or a pill

roads schools bridges

closed

churches stores

neighbors helping to dig out

the white

drifts swallowing

marble steps

the Capitol

teased into a sledding hill

in bright coats

we lay down

and make angels

on this day

no dog bites no

bee stings

no inalienable rights taken

no shootings just

flakes like ashes

from a feverish world

gentling down

on our noses

and eyelashes

IV

Backyard Journal

July again. Birds are warbling a language it seems
I've forgotten, the PIN to an account
rich with epiphanies, like a side trail to a clearing
fringed and fat with dewy raspberries.
Old desires lie dormant within me
while I stare into the back forty.

The flowers of the trumpet vine and the ruby-throated
visitor delirious with nectar hear this:
beneath layers of wingbeats,
of twittering insect chant
and the inhale-exhale of this human observer,
a molecular hum blends and blurs.

So this is the world of the 10,000 things.
The magazine in my lap casually relays
a sample from Hubble's ultra-deep field:
uncountable galaxies bloom in the garden of the outer dark—
whirlpools, sombreros, crab and cat's-eye nebulae.
Before I can finish my coffee, our star's luminous body
is over the weeping willows. Geese honk. Silver maples
sigh in a breeze that flaps these pages, and I am back
to the illusion of discrete thought and landscape,
the separation of this from that.

LANDSCAPE WITH TWO FIGURES

Whatever soreness is
in my body when I rise
from picking snap peas
and hauling irrigation lines
in the midday heat
to look at you across the strawberry field
is a signal flare, a gulp
of swallows lifting all at once,
sweeping through the light.

Cheat River

Tonight
on the bridge where I miss you most
I cast a line

to the river

The moon shimmers
like a fish scale

or a ten-penny nail
a hand holding a hand

::

It's true

With a line and enough patience
you can feed
your friends

::

Once we lay in the grass
shined up and watching
something
called Summer
Moon in the sky
Moon on the river

For a second it looked
blood-dusk-amber
like the ventral fins of perch

like our eyes
closed facing up

It was only
the bottle light

::

The big ones feed
down where the bank deeps off
in the darkness
where the little ones are scared to go

::

I love to look
at hearts
said the boy

I slit our trout
tail to jaw
on some newsprint

I laid its parts
on the paper
to show him

Monongahela

The pickup parked on Main Street full of moose
belongs to the guy sitting in the diner booth
with apple pie and cheddar on his plate.

No one dares touch it, though
we gather 'round the bed the way folks do
at county fair when blue-ribbons get paraded.

And though this heap of flesh animating dusk
with a halo of swarming flies
has no names to mark its flank, no words

to flag the region of fine hairs near its marbled eyes,
nor the provinces of long and tapered legs
it once used to clamber—clumsily, gracefully—

up slopes of birch and spruce, the body's stillness
offers access: a topography ripe with thresholds
to imagined existence. Its ample form reminds me

of an enormous raised relief map I'd seen as a boy
in West Virginia: the Monongahela Forest dwarfed,
housed in glass. Brierpatch Mountain to Spruce Knob,

the wimpled earth swirled with contours, a work done
in great blotches of green and beige and brown,
revealing lookouts, balds, and creek gullies. I began there—

Ketterman Knob, Timber Ridge, Sinks of Gandy—
and followed the easy slip into remoteness, possibility.
Red switchback roads, little clutches of black

(Elkins, Harman, Whitmer, Judy Gap),
the North Fork of the South Branch
running blue into the heart: old place

I am forever returning. Carry me back.
In the afterglow of evening in this village in Vermont,
Butternut, Whiteface, and Madonna peer

into the truck bed like some perverse nativity
as the wind unhinges a skein of scarlet leaves
that swirl and light onto the hide.

Gloaming smolders to night
and the lines of moose are lost to shadows.
I walk away, speaking the names

that let me wend again through that land
of slantwise tobacco barns, silviculture,
endless extractions.

Mount Hunger

There is a certain ease of mind
I get from reading the same poem

over and over, the way I might choose
the same trail up a mountain, following

its contours, lines steep and lush
with berry tangle and moose maple,

to a place among sentinel pines
and cloud drift. Again and again

I find myself there noticing the changes—
Work of the brook upon bedrock, ancient

in its patience, trailside ferns unfurling
from fetal coil to full feather, split

trunk of a hemlock lightning struck
like a thought shuddering and splintering

to the ground underfoot—
following discernible print

to where I can shed the self
like a bright snake sloughing

its skin along a rock shelf.
Pearly delicate translucence

thin as a dream in which I'm lost again.
A partridge bursts from within

my own heart—wild drumming
at the margins.

A WILD PERFECTION

To shirk the heavy weather
we waded in the river, watching Avery
turn rocks in search of salamanders,

crawdads in the murk and such,
another hunk of shale to chuck and cause
the minnows to skitter under surface.

A blue bunch of clouds tumbled
in from Jones Mountain and brought
the smells of mud and summer water.

In the roll of thunder he wandered
off to dare the riffles; he wouldn't listen.
You stumbled after, over stones underfoot

and scooped your dripping, giggling son
into your arms. He flailed like a bream, yelped
his boy cry, then bolted into the greenbrier

quick as a weasel. If only we could
all run widdershins back to some Saturday
afternoon along a stretch of river

before rivers spoke a tongue
of polychlorinated biphenyls, heavy metals,
aluminum, valleys gone to rust or ruin,

it might resemble this thin rush of clear-
seeming water and flakes of sky reflected.
And a clown prince, lord of his own radiance,

sitting in the bushes, pinching blackberries
from a tangle, giddy with the blush
they squirted on his fingers.

Daddy, he said on the winding drive home,
When I was a fish, I lived in that river.

Heirlooms

In gardens we fall
in love with what grows:
heirloom harvests of Brandywines and Oxhearts,
Mortgage Lifters and Big Rainbows,

as if love itself were a green
tomato ripening on the windowsill
of its own momentum,
like dumb luck and not

what brings us to our knees
in rich soil, so that what we lift
from the vine and take inside us

is not only sweet firmness
but back ache and blemish, not just
fine juices but the threat of early frost.
Through thistle and sunlight,
blight year and bounty,
we carry on—this work
of life, this cultivating and caring,

putting up glass quarts of ripe Hearts
that will bear us through December
drifts and longest nights
like a dreamsong of summer.

It will feed us season after season
after ever-fruiting season—
this attention to what grows, this
dedication, this harvest, this labor of love.

The Night We Didn't See

A story made of light
is one thing she wanted to see,

a people's history
in hanging fire.

When we agree that certain points
join in constellation
a picture forms, a kind of clarity.

Imperfect but sufficient,
which is all we have for love.

Behold the northern sky:
a junkyard of wishes,
Greek names, satellites, and bears.

The glow washing up the hill
like an orange tide
was not the rumored aurora

but the campus lamp posts.
Fox cries and filaments
Wi-fi and wet dreams

And what did you want—
confirmation of your smallness?
You are a creature in a body

Little planet
your gravity
little something.

Fields filled with fire-
flies, bodies blinking off
across the grasses—

Off   on   off
through the dark grasses,
indecipherable
as words on a page
in night black night.

THE FIELD

We're down 5-2 and I've been watching fog
creep into the outfield from behind me,
thinking about the way summer

has already made a ghost of itself.
And when the big guy with the neck tattoo,
who's already scorched a double down

the third-base line, nails another one toward me,
I'm not ready. There's no fence to keep the ball
from rolling into the deep and unmowed

corners of the park. So I follow it there
looking for the grass-stained Spalding my dad
and I threw back and forth and back until dusk,

so as to keep out of Papaw Carter's house
that smelled of death, which is to say it smelled
of urine and of raw chicken thawing

on the kitchen counter and the years of
mineral oil worked into the dark
wood furniture of the living room.

One of Papaw's farm cats slinks by. Splash of blood
on its white face. And I am looking for the ball,
keeping my eyes away from the house and

the man in the house who shares my blood.
Whose purpled toes had to be cut off to save
the left foot. Whose purblind pony paced

a circle in the bare grass. Whose papery
voice was kept thin under blankets in August.
When he dies, Mom says his heart will fly

home to Jesus. And I picture the bloody form
like the red bird the cat dragged into
the dooryard, rising over the farm, over

the low grey skies of Pruntytown,
vanishing beyond the mountains.
Papaw died in a room with the TV on

mute. I can't recall what happened
to that swayback pony nor the ball,
nor even where to find the plot

of earth where he's buried.
Someone is crying Home as the big guy rounds
third. Home! I leg it out to the taller grasses

now damp with end-of-summer evening.
And there in the grass is the ball.
Home. It seems impossibly far.

THE PINES

When the last satellite blinks out
we'll be left with only stars again:

the bare sky
and language
our friends

old stories and recitations

::

Where do we go when we go dark?

We collect ourselves among the trees
groping a little with our feet
along the logging roads
skylighted by broken crowns

to earth again
little bivouac
we dreamed by the lake

::

I was born of the water
into light

Just like you

The pines were born of fire
Some of them were crucified
in creosote, strung up
for long-distance utility lines

::

Even with all night forever
all is never lost

While hurt patrols
the hollowed veins of our once cities

our memories, our hearts
will engine what can be kept of us

Your hand in mine
a blessing

Tall pines drink the wind,
hold steady in its paws

::

There is another world
and it's inside this one

Before we became data
each of us a garden

The inch of dirt that keeps us human
Brothers, are you ready?

Ready to go home?

::

We'll gather like new-day monks or moths
A fire between us
Each heart-warm friend
we reckon them one by one
Each name a bead in the bracelet
Each arrival a thanksgiving

In the face of the lake
stars make replicas of themselves
forgetting our names for them

so we can all begin
tender as children
making a new life in the trees

NOTES AND ACKNOWLEDGMENTS

NOTES

Spelter, West Virginia, is a small company town in Harrison County formed in 1910-11 as an immigrant community of zinc-plant workers, mostly Spanish (Asturian). The old Spelter zinc-smelting site was first run by Grasselli Chemical Company, then by DuPont, later by Matthiessen+Hegler Zinc Co., and finally by T. L. Diamond & Co. DuPont operated the zinc smelter from the 1920s to the 1950s, then sold it when an internal report revealed how much air-pollution upgrades would cost. My grandfather, John Walsh, worked in the plant for twenty-eight years before it shuttered its main operations in 1971, when nearly all zinc-smelting in the U.S. was outsourced overseas.

In 2001, the smelter site was shut down completely. DuPont worked with state regulators to demolish the factory and cap the 112-acre site in 2002-2003. Spelter resident Rebecca Morlock discovered that seepage from the reclaimed site was leaking into the West Fork River, and in 2007, a group of residents successfully sued DuPont for corporate negligence that had exposed thousands of area residents to dangerous levels of arsenic, cadmium, and lead. The $382-million verdict for damages (the largest civil penalty ever levied against DuPont) was appealed to the State Supreme Court. In 2010, the parties reached a settlement. DuPont agreed to fund a thirty-year medical monitoring program for current and former residents, including myself and my family, to ensure that any effects from exposure would be discovered in a timely fashion, and to pay $70 million to remediate the surrounding properties and kick-start the medical monitoring fund, which commenced in 2014.

Although many of these poems draw upon my own and my family's experiences in Spelter, the individual people named are often fictionalized amalgamations.

"Expert Testimony (Perrine v. DuPont, 2008)" is lifted from part of the testimony of plaintiff expert witness and soil scientist Dr. Kirk Brown, which is available here: http://www.courtswv.gov/supreme-court/docs/spring2010/34333.htm

::

"The Lee Shore" is for Michael Dickman and for Bulkington, Herman Melville's character in *Moby-Dick*, who is described as being "one of those tall mountaineers from the Alleganian Ridge in Virginia." Whale oil was a common source of lamp light until the dawn of the petroleum era in 1859 in Western Pennsylvania quickly replaced it with kerosene, coal, oil, and natural gas.

"Now Comes Good Sailing . . . ": In his biography, *Henry Thoreau: A Life of the Mind* (University of California Press, 1986), Robert D. Richardson writes that Thoreau's "last words came back to his writing. Early in the morning on May 6 [1862], [his sister] Sophia read him a piece from the 'Thursday' section of *A Week*, and Thoreau anticipated with relish the 'Friday' trip homeward, murmuring, 'Now comes good sailing.' In his last sentence, only the two words *moose* and *Indian* were audible."

"The Cloud" is for Adam Fell.

"A Wild Perfection" is for Sebastian Matthews and his son, Avery Climo Matthews.

ACKNOWLEDGMENTS

Thanks to the editors of the following journals, where some of these poems first appeared, sometimes in different versions or with alternate titles:

Blackbird: "Reckoner"
Ecotone: "Monongahela" (as "Geography")
FIELD: "The Lee Shore"
Forklift, Ohio: "Before the Word" and "The Cloud"
Green Mountains Review: "In the Frame of Innings, Pendleton County, WV" and "Reading"
Ink Node: "Blind Lemon Something" and "The Pines"
jubilat: "Day of Reckoning"
Narrative: "Pruntytown," "A Wild Perfection," "Self-Portrait with Exile, Bears, and the Original Carter Family," and "Spelter, WV (Unincorporated)"
The Oleander Review: "'Now Comes Good Sailing . . .'" (as "The Maine Woods")
The Southeast Review: "Ghost Factory"
Southern Poetry Review: "Sinks of Gandy" (as "Here")
Thoreau Society Bulletin: "Mount Hunger"

"The Field" also appears in the anthology *Eyes Glowing at the Edge of the Woods: Fiction and Poetry from West Virginia* (West Virginia University Press, 2017). Thank you, Doug Van Gundy.

Thirteen of these poems appeared in *The Sinks* (winner of the 2010 Mississippi Valley Poetry Chapbook contest, selected by Jennifer Perrine, MidWest Writing Center Press).

"Reckoner," "The Cloud," and "The Pines" were published in a letter-press edition chapbook by Chickadee Chaps & Broads in 2015. Thank you, Julia Shipley.

I am grateful for my many generous teachers, especially A. Van Jordan, Stanley Plumly, Amaud Jamaul Johnson, Ron Wallace, Amy Quan Barry, Jesse Lee Kercheval, and Jean Valentine.

Thank you to Warren Wilson College, the MFA Program at the University of Wisconsin-Madison, the Bread Loaf/ORION Environmental Writers' Conference, and the Vermont Studio Center for nurturing my own work and the creative lives of so many people. Thank you to my astonishing students and colleagues over the years at the University of Michigan's New England Literature Program (NELP).

::

For their careful reading, fellowship, encouragement, and inspiration, thank you: Curtis Bauer, Ross Gay, Alexander Long, Cate Lycurgus, Matt Hart, Steve Scafidi, Ann Pancake, Gary Clark, Zayne Turner, Laurie Macfee, Nandi Comer, Kerrin McCadden, Baron Wormser, Patrick Phillips, William Brewer, Lisa Russ Spaar, Dara Wier, Evie Shockley, Brian Teare, Vievee Francis, Gabrielle Calvocoressi, Srikanth Reddy, Terry Tempest Williams, Tim DeChristopher, Lisa Kundrat, Barrett Swanson, Nate Brown, David Plastrik, Nick Harp, and Jared Jasinski.

Special thanks always to my poetry family: Michael Dickman & Phoebe Nobles, Adam Fell, and Sebastian Matthews for their unfailing support, shoves, and friendship. And to Nels Christensen & Jess Roberts for the remarkable Superior Street Residency—so much love and gratitude!

Thank you to my family, particularly my Uncle Tom (John Thomas Walsh, Jr.) who was an invaluable resource in sharing his experiences working at the Spelter zinc plant.

Thank you to Laura Wetherington, Christine Kelly, and the whole team at Baoab Press for believing in this book.

Katie Grauer, my heart is full of song for you—wild and wonderful!

Biography

Photo Credit: ©Bradd Celidonia 2019

Ryan Walsh was born and raised in West Virginia. He is the author of two chapbooks, *Reckoner* (2015) and *The Sinks* (winner of the 2010 Mississippi Valley Poetry Chapbook Contest), and his poems have appeared in many journals, including *Blackbird, Ecotone, Field, Forklift, Ohio, Green Mountains Review,* and *Narrative.* He earned an MFA from the University of Wisconsin-Madison and a BA from Warren Wilson College, and he has received grants and scholarships from the Vermont Arts Council and Bread Loaf Writers' Conference. He has taught creative writing and literature at Albion College, University of Michigan, University of Wisconsin-Madison, and at the Champlain College Young Writers' Conference. After working at Vermont Studio Center for many years, where he directed the writing residencies program, he now lives in Pittsburgh, Pennsylvania.

The body of *Reckonings* is set in Times New Roman, a serif typeface designed for legibility in body text. It was commissioned by the British newspaper *The Times* in 1931 and conceived by Stanley Morison, the artistic advisor to the British branch of the printing equipment company Monotype, in collaboration with Victor Lardent, a lettering artist in *The Times'* advertising department.

The headers of *Reckonings* are set in Trajan Pro 3, a display serif typeface released in 1989 and developed by Carol Twombly and Robert Slimbach for Adobe.